DISCOVERY PLAYBOOKS
Hot and Cold

ELIZABETH LAIRD

Educational Consultant: **Carole Ritchie**

Illustrated By **Clare Beaton**

A Piccolo Original
Piccolo Books

This series has been prepared in consultation with the Pre-school Playgroups Association.

Billy's got a temperature

Poor Billy's not very well.
He's got chicken-pox.
He's covered with spots and he's feeling cold.
'Can we get him a hot water bottle to warm him up?' asks Susie.

How do you warm yourself up when you feel cold in bed?

Now Billy's too hot.
Mum turns off the radiator and takes his temperature with a thermometer.
'I'll get you a nice cold drink,' says Susie.

How do you cool yourself down when you feel too hot?

Some food needs to stay cold

Susie gets some orange juice out of the fridge.
Brr! Everything in the fridge feels cold.

Did you know that coldness stops food going bad
and keeps vegetables crisp and crunchy?
What kind of food do you keep in your fridge?
And what do you keep in the food cupboard?

Susie opens the freezer.
She pops two lumps of ice into Billy's cup.
'That looks nice,' she says.
'I think I'll have some myself.'

What happens to ice if you take it out of the freezer and forget to put it back?

Warm clothes for cold weather

Susie and Dad are going to the shops
to get some lotion for Billy's spots.
Susie's put on her party shoes
and her best dress and her new hair slide.
'You can't go out like that,' says Dad.
'You'll have to wear boots and gloves
and a hat.'

'No!' shouts Susie. She's furious.
'Come on, love,' says Dad. 'It's freezing outside.'
Susie grumbles, but she does what Dad says.
She puts on her warm coat, and her gloves.
She knows Dad won't take her if she doesn't.

What do you wear when you go out in the cold?

Ice and frost

Wow! It really is cold!
Susie can see her breath coming out in big puffs.
There's an icicle on the railings,
and fringes of white frost round the fallen leaves.
Susie jumps on a frozen puddle. The ice cracks.
It makes a creaking, snapping noise.

Susie takes off her gloves and picks up some ice, but she soon drops it again. It's so cold it makes her hands ache.

Have you ever been out in really cold weather? How long can you hold a piece of ice before your fingers start to ache?

Fire

Just past the chemist's there's a
building site.
The workmen have lit a fire
to burn up some wood.
'Hey, watch out!' shouts a workman,
as the flames leap up.
The burnt wood turns to ash.
The ash is so light that it flies up into
the air.
'I wish I could float about like that,'
says Susie.

The fire's so hot that it's glowing red.
'Can I put something on it?' asks Susie.
'No,' says Dad. 'It's very dangerous.
If you go too near, your clothes might
catch fire.'

Have you ever helped to collect rubbish for a bonfire?
How do you make sure you don't get burnt?

Warming yourself up

It's lovely to be in a nice warm house again.
Susie's toes and fingers are still tingling with cold.
'Jump up and down,' says Mum.
'That'll warm you up.'

What happens to you when you jump up and down?
Does it make you feel hot?

Dad's making some hot chocolate.
Susie likes that when she's been out in the cold.
'Quick, Dad! The milk's boiling over!' calls Susie.

Have you ever seen boiling milk? What does it look like?
What happens if it boils over?

Keeping warm at home

Billy's made himself a little house in his cot.
'I think I'll make an igloo,' says Susie, 'like they have in the frozen north.'
She puts some chairs and cushions together, and covers it all with a blanket.
'Look Billy,' she says. 'I'll be warm in here.'

'Cover up those cracks,' says Mum. 'Or the arctic wind will come whistling in.'

How do you stop the wind whistling into your home?
How do you keep it warm inside?
Have you any heaters? What kind are they?

Energy makes things warm

Susie's tired of igloos. She's chasing a balloon.
'You're full of energy,' says Mum.
'Energy,' says Susie. She likes new words.
'Energy,' she says again. 'What does it mean?'
'It's a kind of power in your body,' says Mum.
'You use it up when you move, and it keeps you warm.'

Why don't you try using up some energy, and see if you get warm?
Rub your hands together very fast. Do they feel warm?
Now run round the room twice, as fast as you can.

Are you feeling warmer?

Cooking

It's nearly time for supper.
Mum's bought a pizza, and
grated some extra cheese.
Susie helped to spread it on top.
In the hot oven, the bits of cheese
will melt and run.

'I can't wait!' says Susie.
'Can I have it now?'
'Yes,' says Mum, 'but let it cool down a bit first.'
Billy's hungry too. He must be getting better.
He'll be his old self again tomorrow.

What are you having for supper tonight?
Have a good look at the food before it's cooked, then look at it again when you're eating.
How has it changed?

Try it for yourself...

Some things melt when they get warm.
Put a little butter on a saucer,
and leave it in a warm place,
near a radiator, or in the sun.
Do the same with a little margarine,
and a piece of chocolate.

Go back and look at them after an hour.
What has happened to them?
Do the butter and margarine look the same
when they've melted?
What's happened to the chocolate?

Now put the three saucers back in the fridge.
Leave then for an hour.
Do they look the same as they did
before they melted?

Now try freezing things.
Put in the freezer a small tomato,
a lump of cheese about the same size,
some milk in a plastic egg cup,
and the same amount of water.
Look at them every quarter of an hour.
Which goes hard first?

Now leave them out of the freezer to melt.
Are they the same when they've melted?
Do you still want to eat the tomato,
and the cheese?
Has the milk changed?
What about the water?

Water slowly disappears
when you leave it in a warm place.
It turns into mist and floats away.
See what happens yourself.
Get a cup. Put into it two spoonfuls of salt
and one of water.
Mix two spoonfuls of sugar and one of water
in another cup.
Now put one spoonful of water in a third cup.
Leave them all in a warm place all night.
What do you find in the morning?

Have fun with ice too.
Put some water on a metal tray,
and leave it in the freezer.
It will turn into a sheet of ice.
Take it off the tray and put it in the sink.
Then turn the tap on,
and hold the ice under the tap.
Wherever the water falls,
it warms up the ice and melts it.
You can make lovely patterns of holes
in the sheet of ice.

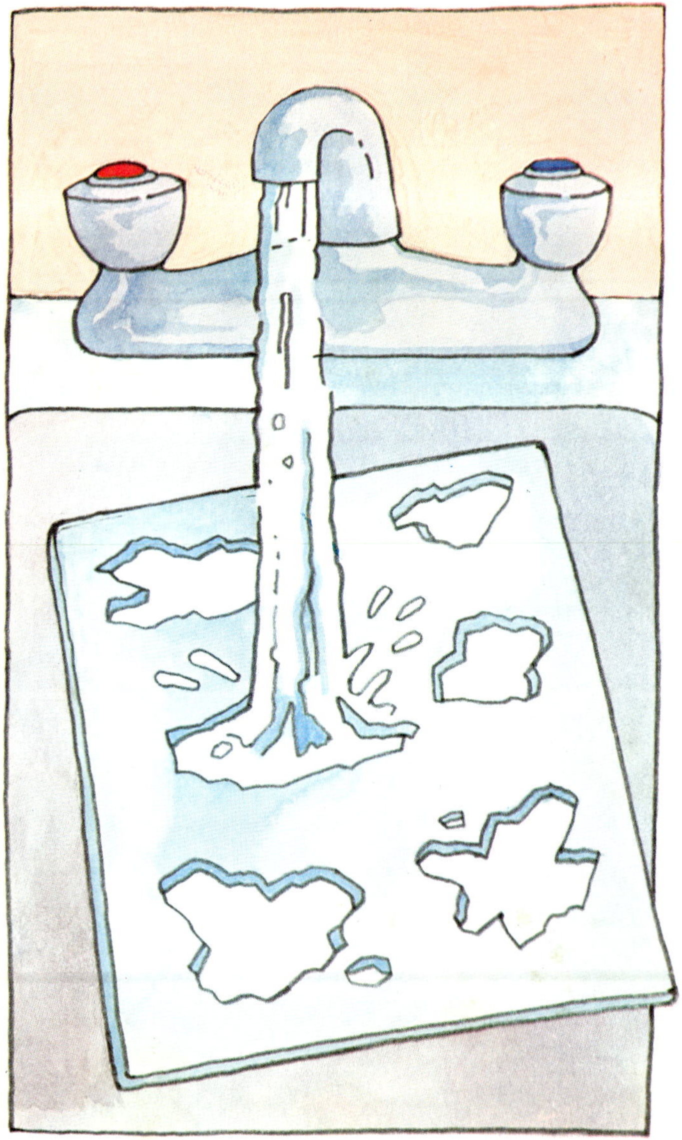